FOODS
in Different Places

Linda Barghoorn

Crabtree Publishing Company
www.crabtreebooks.com

Learning About Our GLOBAL COMMUNITY

Author: Linda Barghoorn

Publishing plan research and development: Reagan Miller

Substantive editor: Crystal Sikkens

Editor: Reagan Miller

Notes to educators: Shannon Welbourn

Proofreader and indexer: Janine Deschenes

Design: Samara Parent

Photo research: Samara Parent

Production coordinator and prepress technician: Samara Parent

Print coordinator: Margaret Amy Salter

Photographs:
Alamy: © Johnny Greig: p11 right

Creative Commons: Joannekinginaddis: p5 top left, p15 bottom

iStock: © PeopleImages: title page; © Jodi Jacobson: p19

All other images by Shutterstock

Front cover: A family enjoys a traditional meal together in China.

Title page: A middle-eastern family enjoys a traditional feast at the end of Ramadan.

Contents page: A girl serves special bread and wears traditional clothing for a Russian celebration.

Library and Archives Canada Cataloguing in Publication

Barghoorn, Linda, author
　　Foods in different places / Linda Barghoorn.

(Learning about our global community)
Includes index.
Issued in print and electronic formats.
ISBN 978-0-7787-2009-6 (bound).--ISBN 978-0-7787-2015-7 (paperback).--
ISBN 978-1-4271-1650-5 (pdf).--ISBN 978-1-4271-1644-4 (html)

　　1. Food--Juvenile literature.　2. Food habits--Juvenile literature.
I. Title.

GT2860.B37 2015　　　　j394.1'2　　　　C2015-903943-6
　　　　　　　　　　　　　　　　　　　　　　　　C2015-903944-4

Library of Congress Cataloging-in-Publication Data

Barghoorn, Linda, author.
　Foods in different places / Linda Barghoorn.
　　pages cm. -- (Learning about our global community)
　Includes index.
　ISBN 978-0-7787-2009-6 (reinforced library binding) --
ISBN 978-0-7787-2015-7 (pbk.) -- ISBN 978-1-4271-1650-5 (electronic pdf) --
ISBN 978-1-4271-1644-4 (electronic html)
　1.　Food habits--Juvenile literature.　I. Title.
　GT2850.B37 2016
　394.1'2--dc23
　　　　　　　　　　　　　　　　　2015026811

Crabtree Publishing Company

www.crabtreebooks.com　　　1-800-387-7650

Printed in Canada/112015/EF20150911

Published in Canada
Crabtree Publishing
616 Welland Ave.
St. Catharines, Ontario
L2M 5V6

Published in the United States
Crabtree Publishing
PMB 59051
350 Fifth Avenue, 59th Floor
New York, New York 10118

Published in the United Kingdom
Crabtree Publishing
Maritime House
Basin Road North, Hove
BN41 1WR

Published in Australia
Crabtree Publishing
3 Charles Street
Coburg North
VIC 3058

Contents

Our Global Community

The world is a big place with billions of people. It is made up of many countries where people live in **communities**. A community is a group of people that live, work, and play in the same area. Together, we all belong to one big global community. All of us in our global community are connected because we all live on planet Earth.

guava fruit, Mexico (page 21)

ARCTIC OCEAN

CANADA

NORTH AMERICA

NORTH PACIFIC OCEAN

U.S.A.

NORTH ATLANTIC OCEAN

MEXICO

COLOMBIA

SOUTH AMERICA

arepas (corn cakes), Colombia (page 16)

Different and Alike

Learning about how people live around the world helps us understand the many ways in which people are the same. It also teaches us to celebrate the things that make us different and **unique**.

In this book you will learn about the kinds of food people eat in different places around the world. Many of these foods are shown on this map.

injera (bread), Ethiopia (page 15)

ARCTIC OCEAN

ASIA

pho (noodle soup), Vietnam (page 16)

EUROPE

FRANCE

NORTH PACIFIC OCEAN

JAPAN

AFRICA

INDIA

NIGERIA

ETHIOPIA

VIETNAM

PHILIPPINES

MALAYSIA

INDONESIA

SOUTH ATLANTIC OCEAN

AUSTRALIA

starfruit, Philippines (page 21)

cassava (vegetable), Nigeria (page 11)

A Basic need

Food is a **basic need**. A basic need is something all people must have to survive. People all over the world need food to grow and stay healthy. Not all people meet their basic need for food in the same way. Some people mostly eat food that comes from plants. Other people get their food from animals.

Food gives us the energy we need to move, learn, and grow.

Hunting and Fishing

The foods people eat depends a lot on where they live. People who live near water often catch seafood, such as fish, for food. In areas with a lot of flat land, many people grow crops. Crops are plants grown for food. In some places, people hunt and eat wild animals.

Japan is a country that is surrounded by water. Many people catch and eat fish and other seafood.

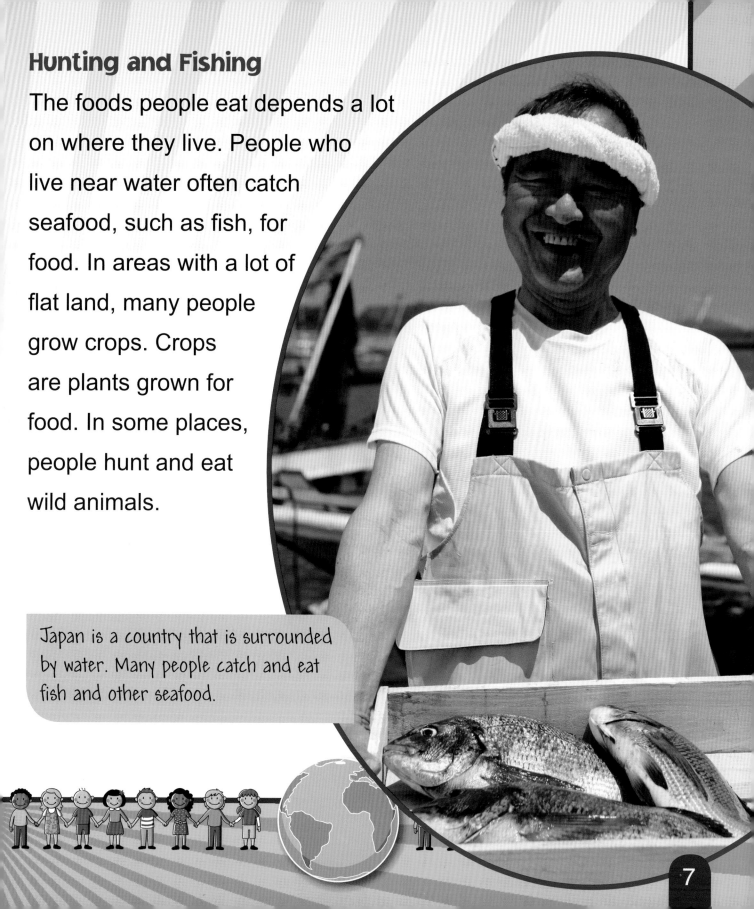

Growing our Food

Farmers are people that grow crops, such as **grains**, rice, fruits, and vegetables. They also raise animals for food. Farm animals give us meat, milk, and eggs. Farmers live in **rural** communities where there is a lot of land for their crops and animals.

Wheat is a grain that is used to make flour. We use flour in many foods, such as bread and pasta.

Food in the City

In cities, or **urban** communities, a lot of people live close together. Most do not have enough land to grow their own food. People living in cities depend on farmers to provide them with the food they need. Farmers sell their food to grocery stores or **markets** where people can buy it.

People in **suburban** communities live just outside the city center on larger pieces of land. Some people are able to plant gardens to grow some of their food.

What Grows Where?

What kind of foods people grow and eat depends on what the **climate** is like where they live. Climate is the usual weather in a certain place. Some places have hot and rainy climates. Other places are often cold and dry. Different foods grow best in certain kinds of climates.

Many parts of India get a lot of rain and hot temperatures for most of the year. Rice is a crop that grows well in this type of climate.

Climate in Different Seasons

In some areas of the world, the climate changes with the seasons. Some areas have four seasons—winter, spring, summer, and fall. Other warmer places, such as Nigeria, have only a wet, rainy season and a dry season. A cassava is a vegetable similar to a sweet potato. It is one of the few crops that grow in Nigeria during both the wet and dry seasons.

cassavas

Cassavas are the main food grown and eaten in Nigeria.

Buying and Selling Foods

Did you know that some of the foods found in your community's supermarkets may have come from other countries? This is because people from around the world trade food and other goods with one another. Goods are things that can be bought or sold, such as food, clothing, and cars. People trade goods so others can have things that are not made or grown in their area.

Goods can be sent to places around the world by truck, train, airplane, or ship.

How We Share

People that live in places with cold winters cannot grow many crops, such as fruits and vegetables, during this season. Farmers that live in places with warm climates can grow these crops all year. They ship their fruits and vegetables to supermarkets in places with cold winters. Indonesia is a country with a warm climate great for growing bananas. They ship bananas to places with cold winters, such as Canada.

In return, Canada may send crops that grow well in colder climates, such as wheat, to Indonesia.

How People Eat

We all need to eat food, but people around the world have different ways of eating. Most people in North America eat their food on plates using **utensils**, such as forks, spoons, and knives. In China and Japan, people eat their food using chopsticks. Chopsticks are thin sticks used to pick up small pieces of food.

This Japanese boy is using chopsticks to eat sushi. Sushi is a meal of small rolls of rice, fish, and vegetables.

Hands-on Eating

In Ethiopia, a type of bread known as *injera* is used as both a utensil and a plate. Stews and salads are placed on the *injera*. Pieces of the *injera* are then torn off and used to scoop up the food. In India, people do not use utensils. They eat most of their food with their hands.

banana leaf

In Malaysia, some foods are served on banana leaves instead of plates.

injera

Another plate or tray is sometimes placed under the *injera* in case the food leaks through.

Meals of the Day

Breakfast is often considered the most important meal because it gives you energy to start your day. The food people eat for breakfast is different in many countries. In Vietnam, a special soup with noodles, known as *pho*, is eaten at the start of the day. In Colombia, *arepa* is a favorite breakfast food. It is a flat corn cake often stuffed with cheese, chicken, or fish.

pho

arepa

A flaky pastry known as a croissant is often served with butter and jam for breakfast in France.

Many families in North America gather for dinner in the evening after school or work.

Lunch and Dinner

Lunch is an important meal in Argentina. It is a long, slow meal where families can spend time together. Many businesses close during lunch time. Most children have school in either the morning or the afternoon. This allows families to share a hot meal in the middle of the day.

Food and Festivals

Culture is the beliefs, customs, and way of life that a group of people share. Culture includes things such as language, religion, clothing, and art. Food is also an important part of culture. During celebrations and festivals in many cultures, special foods are eaten and shared with family and friends.

Eating oysters during the Chinese New Year festival is believed to bring good fortune.

India's festival of lights, Diwali, is celebrated by sharing sweet snacks.

Forbidden Foods

In some cultures, people avoid eating certain foods. Many people who follow the religion of **Hinduism** believe it is wrong to kill an animal for food. Because of this, many **Hindus** do not eat meat. Some other cultures do not eat any food for a short period of time. This is called fasting and is usually part of a religious custom.

Ramadan is a religious holiday for **Muslims**, who follow the religion of **Islam**. Muslims in countries such as Indonesia fast during the day for one month. At the end of Ramadan, people celebrate with a large meal.

Learning About Food

We all need to eat **nutritious** foods to keep our bodies strong and working properly. Learning more about different foods can help us make healthy food choices. Helping to grow your own food in a garden or preparing meals for your family are good ways to learn more about nutritious foods.

Helping to buy food at the supermarket is another good way to learn about different kinds of food.

New Foods

Food is shared all over the world. This gives us a chance to try new foods from different places. Research new nutritious foods and look for some in your supermarket. Have you ever tried a starfruit from the Philippines? How about a guava from Mexico?

guava fruit

starfruit

Notes to Educators

Objective:

This title encourages readers to make global connections by understanding that all people have a basic need for food in order to grow and stay healthy, but the foods they eat are different in various places around the world.

Main Concepts Include:

- food gives us the energy we need to move, learn, and grow
- people often eat food that is dependent on where they live and suitable for growing in their climate

Discussion Prompts:

- Revisit the types of food described in the book. Connect each type of food to the climate or environment in which it is found. Ask readers how each type of food is suited for the climate or environment. How does each type of food compare to what they eat? How is it the same? How is it different?

Activity Suggestions:

- Invite children to choose a food that they have never tried before. Where does this type of food come from? What kind of climate is needed for it to grow?
- Using the food plate or pyramid model, draw and label a meal that includes the new food item they explored.
- Once completed, invite children to present their food drawings.
- Guide students by providing sentence starters such as:
    - The food that I had never tried before was _____.
    - The type of climate it grows in is_____.
    - It is part of the _____ food group.
    - Other foods that would go well with it are: _____, _____, _____, and _____.
- Encourage children to point out the different food groups they included in their model.

22

Learning More

Books

Cook, Diana F. *The Kids' Multicultural Cookbook* (Kids Can!). Williamson Books, 2008.

Kalman, Bobbie. *Where does our Food come from?* Crabtree Publishing, 2011.

Kumar, Dr. Nidhi. *Kaya and Sai Explore Chicken Masala: Tasting the Planet one Bite at a Time*. Pura Vida Prose, 2015.

Butterworth, Chris. *How did that get in my Lunchbox?* Candlewick, 2013

Hollyer, Beatrice. *Let's Eat!: Children and their Food around the World*. Frances Lincoln Childrens Books, 2005.

Websites

http://kidworldcitizen.org/recipes/
Click on pictures to see a recipe for a traditional food from that country.

www.2learn.ca/kids/listSocG3.aspx?Type=6
Click on 'Don't Gross Out the World' to take a quiz about food cultures around the world.

www.foodnetwork.ca/global-eats/photos/kids-school-lunch-around-the-world/#!India-e1425397688209
Twelve childrens' lunches from around the world in pictures and text.

Glossary

Note: Some **boldfaced** words are defined where they appear in the book.

grains [greynz] (noun) Hard seeds that grow into foods such as wheat

Hinduism [HIN-doo-iz-uh m] (noun) A widespread religion mainly in India

Hindus [HIN-duh s] (noun) Individuals who practice the religion of Hinduism

Islam [is-LAHM] (noun) A religion that follows the teachings of Muhammad

markets [MAHR-kit s] (noun) Public places for buying and selling goods

nutritious [noo-TRISH-uh s] (adjective) Describing something healthy that allows your body to grow

rural [ROO-R uh l] (adjective) Describing something that belongs to the countryside

suburban [suh-BUR-buh n] (adjective) Describing something that is part of a smaller community close to a city

unique [yoo-NEEK] (adjective) Something that is unlike anything else; on its own

utensils [yoo-TEN-suh l s] (noun) Items used commonly in kitchens for picking up food to eat

A noun is a person, place, or thing. An adjective tells us what something is like.

Index